IRISH

For centuries the Irish have mixed wit with
wisdom, as they have porter with whiskey
and to the same intoxicating effect!
This book contains the essence of Irish wit – on
love, religion, the 'hard stuff', the English, with a
generous mix from Behan, Yeats, Swift, Moore,
O'Casey, but above all from 'yer man', the authority
on everything that grows, breeds, breathes,
thinks or computes in the land.

Dedication

To my mother and father, who appreciate
the value of a good story

SEAN MCCANN has written twenty-five books on a
wide range of subjects, from children's fiction to
gardening. He was features editor at Dublin's *Evening
Press* from 1962 to 1988, and works as a columnist for
a number of international publications. Wine and
roses are his main interests and he has won many
international prizes for rose growing. He has lectured
on creative writing and on rose growing in many parts
of the world, including Australia, New Zealand,
Canada and the United States.

OTHER BOOKS IN THE
WIT OF IRELAND SERIES

The Wit of Oscar Wilde
Dublin Wit
The Wit of Irish Conversation

IRISH WIT

Religion, the Law, Literature, Love, Drink, Wisdom and Proverbs

Sean McCann

Cartoons by Tom Mathews

THE O'BRIEN PRESS
DUBLIN

This edition first published 1990 by The O'Brien Press Ltd.,
20 Victoria Road, Dublin 6, Ireland.
Tel: +353 1 4923333; Fax: +353 1 4922777
E-mail: books@obrien.ie
Website: www.obrien.ie
Reprinted 1991, 1996, 1997, 2002.

Originally published 1968 by
Leslie Frewin Publishers Ltd., London.

ISBN: 0-86278-227-9

British Library Cataloguing-in-Publication Data
A catalogue reference for this title is available from
the British Library.

5 6 7 8 9 10
02 03 04 05 06

The O'Brien Press receives
assistance from

The Arts Council
An Chomhairle Ealaíon

Typesetting, editing, layout, design: The O'Brien Press Ltd.
Cartoon illustrations: Tom Mathews and others.
Cover separations: C&A Print Services Ltd.
Printing: The Guernsey Press Co. Ltd.

Contents

Introduction

THE GREATEST WIT in Ireland is 'yer man'. He is also the finest humorist as well as being the leading authority on everything that grows, breeds, breathes, walks, thinks or computes in the land. No one doubts the authenticity of the word of 'yer man'. He is Yeats, De Valera, Wilde, Behan, *Dublin Opinion* and Paddy the Irishman rolled into one. He is the greatest asset to a land that is notorious for its tender toes ... because he has the magnificent advantage of never being held responsible for anything he says or does.

Among the Irish 'yer man' is the maker of laughs ... the man O'Casey had in mind when he said that the Irish thinking is as sober as the English except that it is always 'given the halo of a laugh'. 'Yer man' is the halo-maker. Side by side with him are men whose witticisms have stuck and will forever be linked with their names. These – plus 'yer man' – present a happily malicious collection, immense enough to scarify anyone who looks deeply at Irish wit.

For century after century the Irish have mixed wit with wisdom, porter with whiskey, all to practically the same intoxicating effect although still retaining a clarity that allows them to tell the truth about life and men. And nothing is funnier than the truth – when you hear it between drinks. For a brief sentence or two – if you put in your own punctuation – read the list a compiler has to contend with ... AE Wilde Goldsmith Kettle Behan O'Casey Barrington Roche O'Connell Father Healy Tim Healy Swift Shaw Le Fanu Gibbings Stephens Moore Yeats Birmingham O'Nolan Joyce Gogarty Doyle Tomelty... and just to complete the A to Z there was Zozimus. But never mind, that's enough names for now.

The width of wit has an obesity that would defy any slimming diet. There is everything from the traditional Bull to the scorpion sting, from soft blatherings to verbal karate.

Swift could be most un-Christian with his cruel and often repellent wit, once even suggesting that a cure for famine was to fatten surplus babies for food. Scorpion-like was Susan Mitchell's suggestion that the reason a Catholic wife could not be buried in her Protestant husband's grave was that 'it might mar the perfection of a Protestant resurrection.' 'Yer man' is seldom in that category ... his wit is generally the good-humoured kind saying 'serious things in a way that seem funny when you see how serious they are.' An English tourist asked 'yer man' what the road from Ballina to Belmullet was like because he had heard it was very rough. 'Well, sir,' he said after a few seconds contemplation, 'it's the sort of road I wouldn't like to have to praise.' And again the soft wit carried off an awkward situation when 'yer man' was asked to recommend one of the two hotels in a southern town. 'Well, it's like this,' he said, 'whichever one ye stay at ye'll wish it had been the other.'

This is the softness that takes the edge off the epithets and sarcasm that seldom give a man a chance to reply. Certainly there has been enough of them all in Ireland through the years. James Stephens said that during his time – the early 1900s – Dublin functioned in a state of verbal excitement for everyone was using prose instead of grammar.

On the other hand there is the Bull – a supposedly Irish form of unconscious humour – one man defined it as the saying that contradicts itself, in a manner palpably absurd to listeners but unperceived by the person who makes it. Less word-locked was the definition the late Richard Hayeard gave to me:

> *I look across the hedge – twelve cows I see,*
> *The night is clear, the moon is at the full,*
> *The twelve are laying silent round a tree*
> *And one is standing; one – an Irish Bull.*

But the most famous definition, attributed to Professor Mahaffy, was that an 'Irish Bull is always pregnant'. A definition that has a lot of truth in it . . . if you see what I mean.

It is often the way things are said that *makes* Irish wit . . . and makes it so embracing. There is no restriction on subject matter. In England the new arrival is warned not to get into any arguments or to make jokes about religion or politics. In Ireland it is the very opposite. No good conversation would be complete without one – or both – of them. And where's the man who would omit the other Irish 'topics'? An English judge, recently reducing an Irishman's sentence for house breaking and larceny from five years to three, justified his decision by saying: 'Most of his previous convictions were for ordinary Irish offences – drunk and disorderly and assaulting the police.' But, of course, Irish offences in England are very different from Irish offences in Ireland. Change the phraseology from 'drunk and disorderly and assaulting the police' to 'a drop of the hard stuff, a bit of devilment and a logical argument' and the whole affair assumes different proportions. And like most good things in this world it's the proportions that matter. . . .

Anyway, whatever your views about the Irish, their Bulls or their malapropisms, their howlers or their distortions, you just cannot get away from the fact that from the mythical Cuchulainn to the far from mythical Behan they have left a treasury of wit. Any collection must, of course, be a very personal affair which will mean that there will always be the fellow who will say: 'Sure he left the best ones out . . . come here till I tell you . . .' And to prove his point he will whisper his own collection which, with Dublin's fine acoustics, will send everyone home asking: 'Did you hear "yer man"?'

SEAN McCANN

The Bull

Louis XIV asked Count Mahoney if he understood Italian.

Yes, please, Your Majesty, if it's spoken in Irish.

*   *   *

An Irish recruit being rebuked by the sergeant for striking one of his companions apologised:

I thought there was no harm in it, sergeant, all I had in me hand was me fist.

*   *   *

Colonel Saunderson, MP, in a violent anti-Home Rule speech in the House of Commons in 1890 said:

I was born Irish and have been so ever since.

*   *   *

An Irish member on one occasion told the House:

Sir, if I have any partiality for the honourable gentleman it is a partiality against him.

* * *

A notice:

House to let for ever – or longer if required.

* * *

An Irish chiropodist's announcement:

I have extracted corns from all the crowned heads of Europe.

* * *

A beggar's blessing:

Long life to you, sir, and may you never see your wife a widow.

* * *

Verdict of an Irish jury:

We find that the man who stole the mare is not guilty.

*   *   *

Tenant Right in Tipperary:

If the landlords and the police were abolished there wouldn't be a nation like Ireland on the face of the earth.

*   *   *

An Irish priest being introduced to his audience:

. . . is known all over the world and other places besides.

*   *   *

The Hon Denis O'Connor, another renowned Bull-maker, went into a draper's shop, and asked the price of a pair of gloves which took his fancy. Thinking the price too high he exclaimed:

I'd sooner let my hands go barefoot for the rest of my life.

*   *   *

A Lord Mayor of Dublin was giving a farewell supper and during the last speech said:

I am making my debut for the last time.

*　　*　　*

A barrister friend of JC Percy was consulted about a will in which a deceased woman left her house:

... to be sold at my death to provide for my future maintenance.

*　　*　　*

A prisoner in a Dublin court to the Justice:

I was sober enough to know I was drunk.

*　　*　　*

Policeman reprimanding an impulsive pedestrian:

Whenever you see a policeman standing in the middle of the street doing nothing he is directing the traffic.

*　　*　　*

An Irishman complaining of the hazards of marriage said:

If I had my time to come again I would never marry so young even if I lived to the age of Methuselah.

*　　*　　*

There was an old beggar in Dublin who used to explain that she was——

the mother of six children and a sick husband.

*　　*　　*

As the Irish beggar said with feeling:

Spare a copper, sir, I am face to face with an empty stomach.

*　　*　　*

Lord Howe used to tell of an Irish sailor who prayed every night:

Lord, I never murdered any man and no man murdered me; so God bless all mankind.

*　　*　　*

In an Irish bank bill of the last century there was a clause:

The profits shall be equally divided and the residue go to the governor.

*   *   *

Sir Edward Carson, the Ulster leader said:

Mr Asquith was like a drunken man walking along a straight line – the further he went the sooner he fell.

*   *   *

Parnell, not famous for either wit or Bull once said:

Gentlemen, it seems unanimous that we cannot agree.

*   *   *

An Ulster MP talking of a case of bad treatment said:

We have to go back centuries for a parallel to such treatment and even then we don't find it.

*   *   *

An Irish politician once described a report as:

A wholly garbled account of what never took place.

*   *   *

An Irish politician speaking of an opponent:

Even if he told the truth I wouldn't believe him.

*   *   *

A well-known Dundalk solicitor once wrote to the Automobile Association:

I regret to say that Mr L . . . has successfully undergone a severe operation.

*   *   *

The Cavan undertaker was annoyed that a rival had got the job of burying a well-known local personage. As the funeral passed by he said to a friend:

If the man in that coffin was alive it's I would have his funeral.

*   *   *

Notice on an Irish railway bridge:

Trains stopping on this bridge to move at the rate of not more than four miles an hour.

*   *   *

An old woman lamenting:

Poor Peter Hogan, I'm afraid he's going to die. He's got thin, oh so thin. My husband is thin and I'm thin but poor Peter Hogan is thinner than both of us put together.

*   *   *

A Waterford council official complaining about sewerage smells:

The smells you don't smell are the smells that do you most harm.

*   *   *

At an exhibition in Dublin some years ago of a model of an African village, an old woman was heard to say:

Thank God I was born at home.

*   *   *

Letter from a Dublin firm:

We beg to inform you that all vacancies are full.

*   *   *

A co-operative association according to JC Percy was:

A combination of men with no money who meet each week to distribute it.

*   *   *

Ulster MP in an Orange Day speech:

I look forward to the day when the British Lion will march down the Shankill Road arm in arm with the Statue of Liberty.

*   *   *

'Newry Telegraph':

When they stood up to sing, there was not an empty seat in the whole sacred building.

*   *   *

As a woman rushed with a kettle to pour the water over some burning curtains, her husband shouted at her:

Don't be a fool, Mary, sure that water's no good – it's boiling.

* * *

Some comments:

An Irishman is never at peace except when he is fighting.

Once they abolish hanging in this country they will have to hang twice as many.

She lay at death's door and the doctor pulled her through.

* * *

The greatest Bull maker of all was Sir Boyle Roche. He left an absolute herd behind him and for that alone deserves this spot to himself:

Mr Speaker, how could I be in two places at once unless I were a bird.

I answer in the affirmative with an emphatic 'No'.

Half the lies our opponents tell about us are not true.

Anyone who wishes to diminish the brotherly affection of the two sister countries is an enemy of both nations.

I should have answered your letter a fortnight ago, but I didn't receive it until this morning.

Single misfortunes never come alone but the worst of all misfortunes is generally followed by a greater.

While I write this, I hold a sword in one hand and a pistol in the other.

I concluded from the beginning that this would be the end of it, and I see I was right, for it is not half over yet.

Last Thursday notice was given that a gang of rebels were advancing here under the French standard. Fortunately the rebels had no guns, except pistols and pikes, and as we had plenty of muskets and ammunition we put them all to the sword. Not a soul of them escaped except some of them that were drowned in an adjacent bog; and in a very short time there was nothing to be heard but silence.

The cup of Ireland's miseries has been overflowing for centuries and is not yet full.

All along the untrodden paths of the future I can see the footprints of an unseen hand.

Little children who could neither walk nor talk were running around the streets cursing their Maker.

With trial by jury I have lived and, thank God, with trial by jury I shall die.

* * *

Sir Boyle was suffering from an attack of gout, and thus rebuked his shoemaker:

Oh! you're a precious blockhead to do directly the reverse of what I desired you. I told you to make one of the shoes larger than the other, and instead of that you have made one of them smaller than the other.

* * *

Arguing for the Habeas Corpus Suspension Bill in Ireland, Sir Boyle said:

It would be better, Mr Speaker, to give up not only a part, but, if necessary, even the whole of our Constitution, to preserve the remainder.

* * *

This is how Sir Boyle proposed to guard the Shannon:

Sir, I would anchor a frigate off each bank of the river, with strict orders not to stir; and so, by cruising up and down, put a stop to smuggling.

*   *   *

Fearing the progress of revolutionary opinions, Sir Boyle once drew a frightful picture of the future, warning honourable members that the House of Commons might be invaded by ruffians who, said he:

Would cut us to mince meat and throw our bleeding heads on that table, to stare us in the face.

In Court

A Cork man appeared on a very serious charge and was not represented by counsel. 'You know this is a most serious case,' said the judge, 'are you sure you have no counsel?'

I'm sure, your honour. I have no counsel but you'll be glad to hear that I have some very good friends on the jury.

*   *   *

A man charged in Clare court with stealing a hay fork was told that the prosecution could produce two witnesses who saw him do it. He replied:

Well, I can find a dozen who didn't.

*   *   *

'*The case is proved,*' *said the judge,* '*we award your wife* £1 *a week.*' *The husband:*

That's very kind of your honour, I'll try and give her a few bob meself.

* * *

A lawyer was challenging a doctor's evidence:

Lawyer: Doctors sometimes make mistakes.
Doctor: The same as lawyers.
Lawyer: But doctors' mistakes are buried six foot under.
Doctor: Yes, and lawyers' mistakes sometimes swing in the air.

* * *

A Carlow man charged with assault was asked whether he was guilty or not:

How can I tell your honour, till I have heard the evidence?

* * *

The District Justice, looking at the bulky manuscript in a witness's hand, remarked: '*Could you not give us the gist of it?*' *To which The witness replied:*

It's all gist, your honour.

* * *

Cross-examining a witness in a case where the illegal sale of drink was the charge a lawyer said: 'Did you give him drink from the motor car?'

Witness: I did not.
Lawyer: Did you give him drink from a glass then?
Witness: I did.

* * *

The discussion in court was about a fatal dose of poison given to a horse. Lord Morris was on the bench: 'The twelve grains you gave,' he said to the doctor, 'wouldn't that kill the devil himself if he swallowed it?'

I don't know, my lord, I have never prescribed for him.
Ah, no, doctor, indeed you haven't – the ould boy is still alive.

* * *

A judge insisted on holding a court in a small Irish town on Good Friday despite objections. Commented a lawyer:

Well, your lordship, you'll be the first judge to sit on this day since Pontius Pilate.

* * *

27

From 'The Old Munster Circuit' by Maurice Healy, KC:
Judge Peter O'Brien was regarded as one of the gay sparks of the
bench and a pretty witness could often turn the case before him. On
one occasion, barrister Paddy Kelly was endeavouring to bolster a
weak case by reading the most romantic parts of the correspondence.
After a while Peter lifted a deprecating hand and lisped with a
melancholy smile:

Mithter Kelly, Mithter Kelly, it won't do; it won't do at
all. There wath a time when thuch thingth interethed me;
but I regret to thay I am an exthinct volcano!
Kelly: Begor, me Lord, I think there's a r-rumble in the old
crater yet!

*   *   *

The foreman of an Irish jury returned to say:

. . . that they could not reach a verdict as he had eleven
stubborn brutes to deal with.

*   *   *

John Parsons was travelling with the merciless Lord Norbury,
known as the Hanging Judge. Passing a gibbet, Norbury chuckled
at Parsons: 'Where would you be now if that gallows had its
due?'

Riding alone, my lord.

*   *   *

Judge Norbury could never resist the chance of a grim jest, even when wearing the black cap. To one unfortunate sentenced to hang for stealing a watch:

Aha, you rascal, you reached for time but grasped eternity!

*　　*　　*

Irish court crier:

All ye blackguards who aren't lawyers leave the court.

*　　*　　*

'Have you anyone in court who can vouch for your reputation?' asked the judge. 'Indeed I have, your honour,' replied the accused, 'the Chief Constable.' The police chief was amazed: 'I don't know this man,' he protested:

There you are, sir, I've lived in the same district as the Chief Constable for twenty years and he doesn't even know me . . . isn't that recommendation enough?

*　　*　　*

Boisterous Irish witness when asked if he knew where he was:

I'm in court where you dispense with justice.

*　　*　　*

Digby Seymour was carrying on a conversation during the hearing of a case. The judge was annoyed and said: 'Please Mr Saymour, be quiet.' 'My name is not Saymour,' corrected Digby, 'it is Seymour.'

Well, sir, see more and say less.

* * *

District Justice: Who is appearing for you, my man?
Old farmer: I'm appearin' for myself, sir.
District Justice: Are you pleading guilty or not guilty?
Old farmer: I'm innocent, sir. Sure, if I was guilty I'd have a lawyer.

* * *

F E Smith (later Lord Birkenhead) was cross-examining a nervous little Irishman in the witness-box:

Smith: Have you ever been married?
Witness: Yes, sir. Once.
Smith: Whom did you marry?
Witness: A – er – a woman, sir.
Smith: Of course, of course. Did you ever hear of anyone marrying a man?
Witness: Yes, sir – my sister did.

* * *

A well-known District Justice was sitting in the lounge of a hotel on a hot day drinking a steaming cup of coffee. A close friend arrived and said: 'Why don't you drink something cooling? Have you ever tried chilled gin and tonic?'

No, but I've tried a lot of fellows who have.

* * *

Daniel O'Connell, lawyer, patriot and politician, describing a witness:

She had all the characteristics of a poker except its occasional warmth.

* * *

A friend who asked O'Connell for his autograph got this hand-written reply:

Sir, I never send autographs, Yours, Daniel O'Connell.

* * *

O'Connell didn't always get the better of arguments. Once meeting a friend who was sporting a large pair of whiskers he asked: 'When do you intend to place your whiskers on the peace establishment?'

When you put your tongue on the civil list.

* * *

'*Could you direct me to an honest lawyer?*' asked a woman who stopped O'Connell in the Four Courts. Daniel took off his hat, scratched his head, and said:

Well now, ma'am, that beats me entirely.

The Hard Stuff

A priest to a bride holding up a sozzled groom at the altar: 'Take him away and bring him back when he's sober.'

But please, your reverence, when he's sober he won't come.

* * *

An Irishman's toast to an Englishman:

Here's to you as good as you are; and here's to me as bad as I am. But as good as you are and as bad as I am, I am as good as you are as bad as I am.

* * *

Sheridan, dining with some friends, rose when the brandy was being brought in. 'Now, gentlemen,' he said, 'are we to drink like men or beasts?' In accord came the answer, 'like men.'

Right, let's get drunk; beasts always know when they've had enough.

* * *

Lady Collector to Mrs Casey in Dublin's Gardiner Street: 'I'm collecting for the drunkards' home.'

Then come round about ten o'clock and collect Casey.

* * *

Customer: I'll have an Irish cocktail, please.
Bartender: What's that?
Customer: It's half a whiskey with another half added.

* * *

There was the old club man in St Stephen's Green who always drank his whiskey with his eyes closed. Asked to explain his strange habit he said:

It's like this, whenever I see a glass of whiskey my mouth waters and I don't care to dilute it.

* * *

Sir Edward Carson to defendant: Were you intoxicated?
Defendant: That's my business.
Carson: Have you any other business?

* * *

The local priest seeing a parishioner staggering home drunk commented. 'Ah, Jamesy, I'm afraid you'll find the road you're going longer than you think.'

Sure, Father, it's not the length of the road that worries me but the breadth of it.

* * *

The temperance advocate from Belfast was about to address a gathering in an Orange Hall in County Down. Suddenly there was a lot of tittering among the audience. The speaker, on looking behind, found that he had placed his two posters, 'Alcohol is Poison', 'Water is Best', immediately beside a slogan of the local Orangemen which read:

In Union is Strength.

* * *

Arriving around midnight at a pub in Newmarket-on-Fergus the surprised visitor found the place still doing a great trade. 'When do you close?' he asked the publican.

I would say about the middle of November.

* * *

The renowned Dr Mouillot received a hurried call from a farmer who lived in a Wexford town. He found him suffering from a severe case of pneumonia. 'What have you been doing with yourself at all?' he asked the patient:

Nothing at all, doctor. Yesterday I went to the fair at Ferns and when it was over I walked home. When I reached the house I took off my hat and trousers and hung them on the back of the door and went to bed, but, begob, when I woke up in the morning I was lying in a wet ditch and my trousers were hanging from a branch of a tree.

*　　*　　*

In Limerick lived two poets Sean O'Toumy, and Andrew McGrath – the Merry Pedlar. They fought many battles of wit and verse. O'Toumy once advertised himself in the following lines which are a translation of the Irish he used:

> I sell the best brandy and sherry,
> To make my good customers merry;
> But at times their finances
> Run short, as it chances,
> And then I feel very sad, very.

To this McGrath replied:

O Toumy you boast yourself handy,
At selling good ale and bright brandy,
But the fact is your liquor
Makes everyone sicker,
I tell you that, I, your friend, Andy.

*   *   *

The Dublin woman to the doctor after he had pronounced the cause of her husband's illness:

How could he have water on the brain when he hasn't touched a drop for forty years.

*   *   *

Justice: Do you mean to say that you only had one whiskey?
Defendant: I do, sir.
Justice: And where did you get that one?
Defendant: Oh, at a devil of a lot of places.

*   *   *

An employer to the driver of his delivery wagon: 'Michael, you are looking very rocky this morning.'

Yes, sir, I've a bad headache. I was at a christening last night, sir, an' the kid was the only one in the crowd that took water.

*   *   *

Jacques McCarthy, a famous Irish journalist, once asked for permission to make one final toast at a function before the chairman closed it. Given permission he stood up and said:

Mr Chairman and gentlemen, the toast that I have the honour to submit is that of Absent Friends and with that toast I would like to couple the name of the wine waiter who was supposed to look after me tonight.

*   *   *

A drunk staggered into Bangor churchyard in County Down, and fell asleep among the tombstones. Early next morning a local factory hooter sounded. The drunk wakened up, rubbed his eyes and seeing where he was concluded, not unnaturally, that he had heard Gabriel's Trumpet:

Boys-oh-boys! Not a soul risen but me. This speaks bad for Bangor!

Fighting

An Irish warrior's proverb long before Kipling immortalised it:

Help a woman and hit a man.

*   *   *

An Irish peer of a fighting unit:

I don't know what effect they will have on the enemy, but
by heaven they inspire me with terror!

*   *   *

Dan Donnelly, the great Irish boxer, once advised a novice:

There's no use in life in a man learning to fight unless nature
gave him a bit of a taste for it.

*   *   *

A Dublin man:

I beg your pardon, and that's what no man ever accused me of begging before.

* * *

Elizabeth Fitzgerald surrounded by a vicious army of a neighbouring tribe in the sixteenth century was told that her husband had been captured and unless she surrendered her castle immediately he would be hanged. She stood at the battlements and shouted back:

Mark these words, they may serve your own wives on some occasion. I'll keep my castle; for Elizabeth Fitzgerald may get another husband but Elizabeth Fitzgerald may never get another castle!

* * *

Edmund Burke:

He that wrestles strengthens our nerves and sharpens our skill. Our antagonist is our helper.

* * *

Louis XIV once complained that his notorious Irish Brigade gave him more trouble than all his army put together. One of its officers spoke up:

Please, your Majesty, your enemies make just the same complaint about us.

* * *

Said of the Cork Militia:

They are useless in times of war and dangerous in times of peace.

* * *

From Reminiscences of an Irish Land Agent (1904) *by Samuel M. Hussy: A Mr Scully, a landlord from Tipperary, was the Whig candidate in the Kerry parliamentary election of 1851, and his family was not popular in its own county. A Kerryman, making inquiries of a Tipperary man about him, was answered:*

I don't know this gentleman personally, but I believe we have already shot the best of the family.

* * *

A favourite story of John Costello, former Taoiseach: Two Dublin men were discussing the state of the country. 'The only hope for the country is for us to declare war on the United States,' said one. 'Why so?' asked the other. 'Because they would beat the tar out of us and then, following their usual custom they would be so sorry about it that they would send over millions of dollars to reconstruct the country. And then we'd be better off than we ever were before.' The other fellow took a long draught from his glass and seemed deep in thought. Then he asked:

But where would we be if we won?

*   *   *

A wounded Cork soldier to another:

What are you kicking up such a terrible row over? You would think that there was no one killed but yourself.

*   *   *

There was an Irish soldier who asked his CO for leave saying that his wife was in hospital and there was no one to look after the children. 'Paddy,' said the officer, 'that's strange for I have here a letter from your wife saying that on no account was I to let you home . . . for every time you go you frighten herself and the children.' Paddy replied:

Faith, there's two of the best liars in the army in this room. I was never married in me life.

*   *   *

A soldier was carrying a comrade suffering with a leg wound along the front line when unknown to him a shot knocked the comrade's head off. When the soldier got to the casualty station someone pointed out to him that the corpse lacked a head:

The deceiving creature, he told me it was his leg that was shot.

*   *   *

The soldiers were retreating and one of them shouted across a trench to his companion: 'Come on, Jack Dargan.'

I can't.
Why not?
I've taken a prisoner.
Bring him with you.
He won't come.
Then come without him.
He won't let me.

*   *   *

Epitaph:

Erected to the memory of John Moran, accidentally shot as a mark of affection by his brother.

*   *   *

'Well my good fellow,' said a victorious general to an Irish soldier after a battle, *'and what did you do to help us to gain this victory?'* *'Do '* replied Mike, *'well, sir, I walked up boldly to one of the enemy, and cut off his feet.'* *'Cut off his feet! Why did you not cut off his head?'* asked the general.

Ah! and faith, that was off already.

*　　*　　*

Returned Irish soldier to the gaping crowd, as he exhibited with some pride his tall hat with a bullet hole in it:

See there! Look at that hole, will you? Ye see, if it had been a low-crowned hat, I should have been killed outright.

*　　*　　*

An Irish pilot serving in the RAF, as a piece of flak went through the fuselage on a raid over Germany:

Thank God Dev kept us out of this bloody war!

*　　*　　*

Gentleman to his servant: 'Pat, what's all that noise in the street?'

Oh, nothing, sir; they're only forcing a man to join the volunteers.

*　　*　　*

Three men were in hiding waiting to ambush Lord Leitrim, who was renowned not only for his brutality but also for his punctuality: 'He's late tonight,' said one of the men. Another replied:

I hope to God nothing's happened to the poor gentleman.

* * *

A quartermaster in a regiment of Light Horse, who was six feet high and very corpulent, was joking with an Irishman concerning the natural proneness of his countrymen to make Bulls in conversation. The Irishman replied:

By my soul, Ireland never made such a Bull in all its lifetime as England did when she made a light horseman of you.

* * *

A Kerrywoman, asked who gave her the black eye:

Himself, and who better?

* * *

An Irishman boasted:

... that he had seven sons and had never lifted a hand to one except in self defence.

* * *

A soldier was brought up for stealing his comrade's whiskey ration. His defence was unique:

I'd be sorry indeed sir to be called a thief. I put the liquor in the same bottle his and mine, and mine was at the bottom, and, sure, I was obliged to drink his to get at mine.

Food

Robert Gibbings, a mountain of a man, was once accosted by a tiny Cork woman who looked up from navel height and said:

My God, sir, but you make great use of your food.

* * *

William G Fay, one of the founders of the Abbey Theatre, once toured Ireland with a small circus and reported:

You could get atin' and drinkin' for tuppence a pint.

* * *

Percy French:

I have just come back from a children's party. I am one of the survivors. There are not many of us.

* * *

'*Look at my shoes,*' said the hotel guest, '*look at them. I put them out last night and nobody has touched them.*' The proprietor answered:

That's the sort of hotel we keep, ye might put your gold watch outside and no one would touch it.

*   *   *

'*Bring me a hot plate, waiter,*' said Samuel Lover in a Dublin hotel, '*the beef is good but the plates are cold.*'

Waiter: The hot plates haven't come in yet, sir.
Lover: Well bring them in, man.
Waiter: I mean, sir, they are not in season; hot plates come in in October and go out in May

*   *   *

'*How will you have your eggs cooked?*' asked the waiter. '*Make any difference in the cost?*' inquired Brannigan cautiously. '*No*':

Then cook 'em with a nice slice o' ham, if you plaise.

*   *   *

The visitor to a country hotel asked the waiter for red-currant jelly to go with his mutton:

Beg your pardon, sir, the jelly is all gone, but I can get you some beautiful lobster sauce.

*   *   *

JC Percy thanking a waiter at the Wicklow Hotel in Dublin for bringing him his lunch in a hurry, said, 'You're an angel.'

I am indeed, sir, but I fly low.

*   *   *

Soup kitchens were often used in Dublin during the war. One woman commenting on the standard of the soup available said:

They make it like this – they take a gallon of water and then they boil it down to a pint to make it strong.

*   *   *

JC Percy, author of so many Irish jokes, once remarked to a waiter in a Galway hotel that the weather was very unsettled:

Indeed it is, sir, the glass is hard set catering for it.

*   *   *

When the city folks arrived at the country bungalow they'd rented for the summer they found it had just one flaw – there was no refuse collection. So they bought a pig to consume left-overs, and the arrangement worked beautifully all summer. When ready to return to their city home, they let it be known they had a pig for sale and a prospective buyer enquired the price.

Well, we paid fifty shillings for him, but we've used him all summer. Would twenty-five shillings be too much?'

*　　*　　*

A visitor to Connemara asked a tenant what his farm produced to the acre:

Well, in the summer it might raise enough to feed a hare but in the winter she would have to run for her life.

Literature and the Press

George Russell (AE) once defined a literary movement as 'five or six people who live in the same town and hate each other.' Certainly he was qualified to make the remark – at that time Dublin housed its greatest ever literary movement, a movement that well lived up to his description. Among his contemporaries were Yeats, Gogarty, O'Casey, Martyn, Stephens, Moore, Lady Gregory, Joyce. Much of the verbal karate indulged in has stood the test of time.

Joyce haughtily to Yeats on Yeats' fortieth birthday:

We have met too late, Mr Yeats, you are too old to be influenced by me . . .

*   *   *

Joyce:

Mr Martyn and Mr Moore are not writers of much originality . . . Mr Moore has wonderful mimetic ability . . .

*   *   *

AE to Joyce:

I don't know whether you are a mountain or a cistern but I am afraid that you have not enough chaos in you to make a world . . .

*   *   *

Shaw as he tossed a copy of Ulysses *on the fire:*

I could not write the words Mr Joyce uses.

*   *   *

George Moore, describing how Yeats brought Synge to writing perfection, said:

He stood over him, his pearl pale, or is it his ivory hand, sweeping the strings of a harp of apple wood, rousing a masterpiece out of an abyss.

*   *   *

Robert Farren describing Martyn:

Moore's exotic bucolic.

*   *   *

Martyn refused to read Moore's famous malevolent and entertaining trilogy, 'Hail and Farewell,' saying:

George is a pleasant fellow to meet, and if I read the book I might not be able to meet him again.

*   *   *

Martyn himself described his main recreation in 'Who's Who' as 'George Augustus Moore.' There were times when Moore irritated him more and he wrote:

Moore suffered from mental diarrhoea which had to be shot over his friends.

*   *   *

The most amusing collaboration in the literary movement was described by Moore. Subject for the collaboration was the legend of Diarmuid and Grainne:

Moore was to write it in French; Lady Gregory would then translate his French into English; Taidg O'Donoghue would then translate the English into Irish and then Lady Gregory would translate the Irish into English! After that Yeats would put style upon it . . . !

*   *   *

In 'Hail and Farewell' Moore reprinted some of the French text for this play (Diarmuid and Grainne) – his explanation was:

It was the only way he could convince the reader that 'two such literary lunatics as Yeats and myself existed, contemporaneously, and in Ireland, too . . .'

*   *   *

Moore speaking of his counsin, Edward Martyn, said:

That fellow has no feelings. He quite genuinely believes that I'm damned and he's not even sorry for me!

*　　*　　*

Sarah Purser said about George Moore's 'confession' books 'The Confessions of a Young Man' and 'Memoirs of my Dead Life':

Some men kiss and tell; Moore tells but doesn't kiss.

*　　*　　*

Moore sent a copy of his life of Christ to his friend AE. 'You'll like this better than any of my books,' he wrote. AE replied:

On the contrary, I like it less than any of your books. Jesus converted the world; your Jesus wouldn't convert an Irish County Council.

*　　*　　*

Few writers mocked George Moore more than the beautiful poet and wit, Susan Mitchell. In her life of Moore she devoted one chapter to Moore – the artist. It must be one of the shortest chapters ever published. Here it is:

Nobody in Ireland has ever seen any of Mr Moore's paintings except AE to whom he once slyly showed a head, remarking that it had some 'quality'. AE remained silent.

* * *

Susan Mitchell:

It has been said to me that Mr Moore had enough credulity to make him a bishop.

* * *

Moore once wrote that his brother Maurice was the only member of his family who was a gentleman. To which Miss Mitchell replied:

Mr Moore is an amazingly truthful person.

* * *

Sir Walter Scott was travelling across an Irish ferry and put his hand in his pocket for sixpence for the ferryman. All he had was a shilling. 'Take it, Pat,' he said, 'and you'll give me the sixpence back another time'.

Sure, and may your honour live to get it.

* * *

From Dublin Opinion, *Ireland's leading humour Journal:*

In the old-fashioned novel the hero didn't kiss the heroine until the last page. Now he kisses her on the dust jacket.

Money talks, but you can't hold on to it long enough to start a conversation.

Dear son, I have written to you five times asking you a simple question but I got no reply. What do you think you are? A government department? Father.

George Bernard Shaw's Will

> He left his cash (God help typesetters!)
> To give the alphabet more letters.
> Strange that he should on forty fix
> Who did so well with twenty-six!

A lot of modern upbringing consists of giving children their head and leaving them to find their feet.

A toast! May our country one day become as prosperous as the Income Tax men think it is.

Epitaph
O, shed oval teardrops for Paddy Malone,
Who believed he could wheel a whole scrum on his own!

College Green – where the orator Edmund Burke looks across at the Bank of Ireland, and only the money talks.

The machinery of Government – the taxpayer on a treadmill.

Reason won't stop the next war. It's easier to explode an atom bomb than to explode a fallacy.

* * *

From the 'Irish Times':

The condition of the survivor is rather serious, as he has been severely burned, and also had a fracture of the limbs. He is being removed to Cork under military guard for further medical treatment. An inquest is to be held later.

* * *

Election speech in the 'Limerick Echo':

The poor people always voted for me, and there are more poor today than ever.

* * *

'Cork Examiner':

Exasperated musician to pupil: 'Really, I can't believe that you were born with even drums in your ears.'

* * *

The 'Irish News':

Venus de Milo was the earliest example of a 'hands-off' policy.

* * *

'The Irish Digest':

Lecturer in a village hall: Now, gentlemen, you all know what a monocle is.
Chairman interrupting: Most of us do but perhaps you'd better explain for the benefit of those who were never up in one.

* * *

The 'Irish Independent' (1941):

He (James Joyce) died in Zurich early this year, having in the time between reviled the religion in which he had been brought up and fouled the nest which was his native city.

*   *   *

'Poor Rabbin's Ollminic' was published in Belfast in the mid-nineteenth century – probably the most extraordinary journal ever to come from the North of Ireland. Its dialect humour was unique:

When a man had died and foul play was suspected – 'someone had helped Providence away wi' the crathur.'

The Belfast man wanted a good-looking girl: 'I'd like to marry a girl that is the full o' me eye.'

'Great noise and little wull,' said the Belfast apprentice devil when he tried to pluck a pig.

Thim tha' fights last fights best.

Thim tha' has no cow, kin loss no cow.

Whin ye buy new cannles buy ones made in hot weather; they stand the cold better.

The days of December is now all like Molly Clarke's sweetheart – short and dirty.

Love

Irish proposal of marriage:

How would you like to be buried with my people?

          *   *   *

'The Irish Register', 1742:

Some of our struggling countrymen have, with a small stock of Learning and vigorous constitution, crept into the arms of many a fine woman and an Affluent Fortune.

          *   *   *

Old song:

> Love is the soul of the neat Irishman;
> He loves all that's lovely,
> And loves all he can . . .

          *   *   *

Parthelon, a leader in ancient Ireland found his wife in another man's arms. His wife faced him:

O Parthelon, do you think it is possible for a child and cake, a cat and milk, a bee and honey, or a man and woman to be left alone with one another without them meddling with one another?

*   *   *

A Dublin university professor speaking on the Catholic Church's attitude to sex in 1967 said:

The religious teaching on sex is seen as one which offers a woman a choice between perpetual virginity and perpetual pregnancy.

*   *   *

Frankie Byrne:

Respect is love in plain clothes.

*   *   *

Courtship:

A period during which a girl decides whether she can do better or not.

*   *   *

John Butler Yeats:

Marriage is the earliest fruit of civilisation and it will be the latest. I think a man and a woman should choose each other for life, for the simple reason that a long life with all its accidents is barely long enough for a man and woman to understand each other; and in this case, to understand is to love. The man who understands one woman is qualified to understand pretty well anything.

*   *   *

Oscar Wilde:

A misanthrope I can understand – a womanthrope, never.

*   *   *

Writing of Irishmen who leave it late to get married, Sean O'Faolain said:

I have only four plausible explanations for Irish continence: that sexual desire is sublimated by religion, exhausted by sport, drugged by drink or deflected by either an innate or inculcated puritanism.

*   *   *

An old woman of the house discussing the arrival of a new daughter-in-law on her kitchen floor:

Ay, isn't it a dreadful thing to think of a strange woman puttin' her hand into your tay cannister.

*   *   *

The best way to look at the faults of a pretty woman:

Close your eyes.

*   *   *

The parents had just made a match between their son and the daughter of a well-to-do local farmer. The couple had never met and after the first bringing together the son complained to the father: 'You never told me she was lame.'

Go on outa that, it isn't for racing that you want her!

*   *   *

James Stephens, the poet, once asked George Moore for advice on how to treat two women who would be sitting on either side of him at a formal dinner party:

Don't touch their knees, woman have an instinctive knowledge whether a man who touches her knee is caressing her or only wiping his greasy fingers on her stocking.

*   *   *

The following letter was written by a young Irish farmer:

Dear Miss, I have been in love with you for a long time, and take this opportunity to inform you by letter; and would ye like to cort for marriage? If so, I would like to have you if you are not spoke for. And if you are spoke for, is your sister spoke for? You and she is both so hansom it is hard to tell which is the hansomis. I have got a little farm, an' don't you think I am pretty good-looking. I think you are very good looking. And if you want me an' if you don't want me be sure an' answer me yes or no.

*　　　*　　　*

'O'Brien's had enough, he's making a pass at his wife.'

A young Irishman led a blushing female into the presence of the genial Father Carpenter: 'We want to get married,' *he said;* 'are you Father Carpenter?'

Yes. Carpenter and joiner.

*   *   *

St John Ervine:

Marriage, which is the oldest form of association in human history, has never been perfect, is still imperfect and will always be unsatisfactory. Yet it is our most popular and our happiest wrong.

*   *   *

Donegal girls have the permission of the Pope to wear the thick end of their legs below the knee.

*   *   *

How is your wife getting on, Pat?

Well, sometimes she's better and sometimes she's worse. But from her goin's on when she's better, I often think that she's better when she's worse.

*   *   *

'*I presume, Mrs Murphy, you carry a memento of some sort in that locket of yours?*' '*Indeed I do, sir; it's a lock of my Dan's hair.*' '*But your husband is still alive.*'

Yes, sir, but his hair is all gone.

*   *   *

Mike: Say, Mrs Nolan, I hear you are keeping company with a man, an' your husband is only dead six months.
Widow Nolan: True for you, Mike, I am, an' glad of it.
Mike: Sure, I am ashamed to hear you say so, and indeed you ought to have more respect for his memory.
Widow Nolan: Whist, now, Mike; you can't take a memory in your arms of a cold night.

*   *   *

A Belfast woman summoned her husband for assault. She said he was drunk. He said she was lazy and good for nothing and hadn't given him a decent meal for over a week. 'You're a liar as well,' she shouted at him. 'That I did.'

You did not, an' I can prove it. I pawned the gas stove last Tuesday and you haven't missed it yet.

*   *   *

Bernard Shaw in John Bull's Other Island:

Father Keegan: The more a man knows, and the farther he travels, the more likely he is to marry a country girl afterwards.

* * *

An Irish couple, whose married bliss was not without a few squalls, received a homely lecture from their spiritual adviser regarding their disgraceful quarrels. 'Why, the dog and cat you have agree better than you.' The reply somewhat upset him:

If your reverence'll tie them together, ye'll soon change yer mind.

* * *

When the henpecked husband died and went below, he immediately started throwing his weight around and giving orders to everyone. 'Say, fellow,' roared Satan, 'you're acting as though you owned the place'.

I do! My wife gave it to me while I was on earth.

* * *

Jimmy Hiney, Ireland's great ballad writer, tells this story against himself. A small man, he was taken home to meet his mother-in-law who, looking at him with amazement on her face, said to her daughter:

Well begod if you get nothing else from him you'll always get a laugh.

* * *

Irish bachelor justifying his distrust of marriage:

It took this country seven hundred years to get its freedom – I'm not going to give it up in five minutes!

* * *

The teacher: 'So your name is Johnny Murphy, But your mother's name is O'Brien?'

Yes ma'am. You see, she married again and I didn't.

* * *

Bernard Shaw:

First love is only a little foolishness and a lot of curiosity. No really self-respecting woman would take advantage of it.

* * *

Some Irish opinions:

This is a woman's world. When a man is born people ask: 'How is the mother?' When he marries they exclaim: 'What a beautiful bride.' When he dies they inquire: 'How much did he leave her?'

There is no such thing as confirmed bachelors up to the age of fifty-two – only obstinate ones.

If you marry the right woman there is nothing like it and if you marry the wrong woman there is nothing like it.

Religion

An Irish farmer claimed:

A man in the professions can never lose. A lawyer is paid –
win or lose. A doctor is paid – kill or cure. A priest is paid –
heaven or hell.

*   *   *

*An Ulster man bought a boat named 'Pius the Ninth' from a Wick-
low man. He didn't like the name but could do nothing about it
as it was considered unlucky to change the name of a boat. His wife
was telling a neighbour about the purchase:*

Wife: I'm not well pleased about it. I don't care for who it's
called after.
Neighbour: And who is that?
Wife: Well I wouldn't like to say.
Neighbour: Is it a Roman saint?
Wife: No, it's worse.
Neighbour: Oh Lord, is it a Fenian?

Wife: No, it's still worse.
Neighbour: Lord help us, it must be the devil.
Wife: No, it's even worse than that!

* * *

Advertisement in a Belfast newspaper:

Wanted – man and woman to look after two cows, both
Protestant.

* * *

*A priest once explained why he commanded his parishioners to say
the full Litany of the Saints and not a 'quick' litany:*

I was in the church one Saturday evening, and an old woman
who is on the deaf side and 'whispers' rather loudly, was
praying from her prayer-book this way: 'All the saints on
this first page pray for us . . . all the saints on the second
page, pray for us . . . all the saints on the third page, pray for
us . . . and from all the things on the fourth page, deliver us,
O Lord.'

* * *

Maurice Healy, KC once asked Ulster lawyer John Bartley to explained the difference between a Calvinistic Presbyterian and an ordinary Presbyterian:

I'll tell ye. A Calvinistic Prasb'tayrian believes all you Papishes wull be domned because ye're predastined to be domned; but we or'nary Prasb'tayrians b'lieve all you Papishes wull be domned on yer mer'ts!

*　　*　　*

Oliver Goldsmith:

You can preach a better sermon with your life than with your lips.

*　　*　　*

Pat Hoey, the entertainer, was asked to give a concert in a Carlow town and suggested a fee of three guineas. The parish priest wrote back saying he thought it was a lot and suggested that Pat should make the journey and they would pay him a guinea and promise 'plenty of diversion.' But Pat was not keen. He wrote back:

Dear Rev Father, I am sorry I cannot agree to your committee's terms and incidentally may I, with the greatest respect, submit that anyone who would go to Ballyhillmurray for 'divarshun' would go to hell for fresh air.

*　　*　　*

The parish priest was due to leave the parish and on his last Sunday the parishioners came to wish him well. One lady caught him fervently by the hand:

You are a great man, Father. We knew nothing about sin until you came among us.

* * *

A clergyman was anxious to introduce some new hymn-books to his congregation, so he directed his assistant to make an announcement to that effect immediately after his sermon. But it so happened that the assistant had an announcement of his own to make, as follows: 'All those who have children they wish to be baptised, please hand in their names at once.' The clergyman, who was rather deaf, then arose and said:

And I wish to say, for the benefit of those who haven't any, that they may be obtained from me any day between three and four o'clock. The ordinary little ones are sixpence and the special ones with red backs are one shilling each.

* * *

Dr Salmon, Provost of Trinity College, Dublin, used to tell how his Catholic cook, on contemplating a Protestant kitchenmaid enjoying a beef-steak on Friday, pensively remarked:

If you are not damned for that, all I can say is I have got a queer sell!

* * *

The school – visiting priest: 'With what weapon did David slay the Philistines.' Up came one small hand:

Please, Father, 'twas with the axe of the Apostles!

*   *   *

A Belfast Catholic was asked what was the most pleasant work he had ever done.

Pulling down a Protestant church and getting paid for it.

*   *   *

Asked the priest, of the child: 'What is Baptism?'

It used to be two-and-sixpence, but my mother says it's five bob since you came here.

*   *   *

Sister was explaining to her class the joys and wonders of heaven. After several convincing minutes she asked how many wanted to go to heaven. All but one little girl raised their hands. 'Mary,' Sister asked surprised, 'don't you want to go to heaven?'

I want to go all right, Sister, but my mother told me to come right home after school.

*   *   *

Archbishop Whateley once said:

A preacher should ask himself – am I about to preach because I want to say something or because I have something to say?

*   *   *

Canon O'Connor once asked a child in Kilternan School why did Nebuchadnezzar eat grass?

Because it is written, that he that exalted himself shall be a beast.

*   *   *

The priest asked the child what he understood by an 'unclean spirit'. The child thought for a second, then replied:

Please Father, a dirty devil!

*   *   *

A church member relates:

In our church one afternoon I saw a little boy hurrying down the side aisle. He was clutching something in his fist – a coin, which he dropped into the box. He picked out a votive candle, lighted it, and knelt down. I knelt down, too, about a yard away. He soon noticed me, but at first he kept his eyes fixed on the altar. A few minutes later he leaned over, and in a resentful whisper said: 'You move over. Pray on your own candle.'

* * *

The Bishop of a diocese once stepped in when the local parish priest was taken ill. At the end of his Sunday services a deputation went to thank him:

It was good of your Lordship to help us out today. A worse man would have done but we couldn't find him.

*   *   *

A former priest of Sandymount in Dublin had a fine stocked library but would never loan a book from it. Once a parishioner asked to borrow a book and was told he could – provided it was read in the priest's study. The man declined. A few days later the priest went to the man's house and asked to borrow the garden roller.

Certainly you can, provided you use it in my garden.

*   *   *

There is a story told of Bishop Healy of Galway once going to the local barber for a shave. Unfortunately the barber was recovering from one of his drunken bouts and nicked the Bishop's face badly.
*   'Oh! This cursed drinking!' exclaimed the Bishop. The barber replied:*

Yes, it leaves the skin awful tender.

*   *   *

A letter written home by Sister M Stanislaus McCabe of Carrick-macross:

Sister Mary Oliver wonders how she should address His Eminence Cardinal Gracias, India's first cardinal. You see some people pronounce his name 'Gracious' while others like the Latin word Gratias – Which, she asks, is correct? We told her to say Good Gracious when the Cardinal arrives and Deo Gratias when his Eminence has departed.

* * *

The Belfast Protestant family were getting on the train and the little girl turned and said:

Goodbye God, we're going to live in Dublin.

* * *

Woman, haughtily, to the young shop assistant who was not very helpful: 'Do you know who I am? I'm the Bishop's lady.'

I'm sorry ma'am, but I can't give you a discount even if you were his wife.

* * *

The priest was making a collection for a new church. Said the parish Scrooge:

Put me down for five pounds, Father. And God knows, if I had it I'd give it to you.

*   *   *

The priest and the minister were constant but silent travelling companions. Eventually the minister decided the silence should be broken:

Minister: Good day, Father. We see each other often and I feel we ought to get on speaking terms. After all we're in the same business.
Priest: Indeed, we are. You're doing it your way and I'm doing it His.

*   *   *

Brevity personified are the letters that passed between the Duke of York and the Protestant Bishop of Cork, referring to the ordination of a man named Ponsonby; the Duke wrote: Dear Cork, ordain Ponsonby – Yours York.

The Bishop replied: Dear York, Ponsonby ordained – Yours Cork.

*   *   *

An old Irishman, just recovered from a severe attack of sickness, chanced to meet his parish priest, who had been summoned during his illness to administer the last rites of the church: 'Ah, James,' said the priest, 'I see you out again. We thought you were gone sure. You had a pretty serious time of it.' 'Yes, Father, indeed I did.' 'When you were so near death's door, were you not afraid to meet your God, your Maker?'

No, indeed, Father. The other fellow worried me more!

*   *   *

Father Healy of Bray, Co Dublin, famous for his repartee, when asked what he thought Tim Healy, the famous politician, would be when an Irish Parliament was obtained, retorted:

An old man.

One day he was playing cards with some members of the peerage at the Viceregal Lodge in Dublin, when he took out a handful of coppers. 'Ah, Father,' said one of the young peers, 'I see you've been robbing the offertory box!'

How clever of your Lordship to recognise his own contribution!

Father Healy on food:

Lunch is a poor compliment to breakfast and an insult to dinner.

And on his Bray parishioners:

An ideal crowd – the poor keep all the fasts and the rich keep all the feasts.

The Protestant rector of Bray once said to Father Healy: 'I have been sixty years in the world and I have not yet discovered the difference between a good Catholic and a good Protestant.'

You won't be sixty seconds in the next world until you find out.

He once remarked:

I would prefer Heaven for climate but Hell for society as all my friends are Protestants.

A visiting priest, speaking for a delegation, asked Father Healy – 'We have all been wondering where you got your brilliant gift of repartee from?'

Now that you have inquired, it must have been from my mother – my father was as common as any of you.

The subject being discussed was mistletoe. A woman turned to Father Healy and said, 'This, of course, does not interest you, Father.'

No, not really, we do it *sub rosa.*

A parishioner to Father Healy: 'It's well that you are better.'

Indeed, but it would be better if I were well.

The Protestant vicar of Dalkey was showing his church to Father Healy. 'One thing is sure,' said the vicar, 'my church is built on a rock.'

Yes, a blasted one.

Father Healy was sinking fast, when he was told that an old friend of his was dying! He replied:

I'm afraid then that it's going to be a dead heat.

Sport

During a competition at Hermitage Golf Club a few years ago the secretary saw a competitor about to drive off a few yards in front of the tee box. 'You must not do that,' he said. 'Mind your own business,' said the member. 'I'll have you know I'm the secretary here and it is my job to see that the competition rules are observed. If you hit that ball you are disqualified.' The member ceased addressing the ball and turned bitterly on the secretary:

Again I tell you to mind your own business. I'm playing my third.

*　　*　　*

From 'Dublin Opinion':

The curse of it is that when you're learning golf you hit nothing and when you're learning motoring you hit everything.

*　　*　　*

McCarthy once described the three games of football common to Ireland:

In rugby you kick the ball, in soccer you kick the man if you cannot kick the ball, in Gaelic you kick the ball if you cannot kick the man.

*　　*　　*

One fine morning the Kildare hounds had brought their fox to bay and were killing it on the far side of a stream, too wide to jump and too deep to ride through. The Master was anxious to find out if his hounds were on a dog fox or a vixen, so he shouted across to a man standing on the far side: 'Is it a vixen; is it a vixen?' The man made no reply. The Master shouted again still louder: 'Is it a vixen?' The man shouted back:

How the hell should I know? Sure the dogs have eaten all the sex out of it.

*　　*　　*

Two men were discussing Ronnie Delany's achievement in the Olympic Games. Said one:

He was so fast, that everyone else in the race had to run twice as fast to keep up with him.

*　　*　　*

Asked how many his jaunting car would hold the Killarney man replied:

If you sit contagious it will hold four and if you sit familiar it will hold six.

*   *   *

An Irish horse-dealer is said to have sold a mare as sound in wind and limb and 'without fault'. It afterwards appeared that the poor beast could not see at all out of one eye, and was almost blind in the other. The purchaser, finding this, made heavy complaints to the dealer and reminded him that he engaged the mare to be 'without fault'.

To be sure, to be sure I did, but then, my dear, the poor crater's blindness is not her fault, but her misfortune.

*   *   *

The Galway farmer had just bought a very poor looking horse from a tinker. 'How much did you give for him?' asked his wife. He replied, 'I gave four pound for him.'

You don't tell me! Well you couldn't have got a better one for less.

*   *   *

A man buying a horse from a tinker at Ballinasloe Fair:

Is this a good horse that you're selling me?
For what do you want him?
For sending to England.
Oh he'll do well for that; he's a good horse for exportation;
he's very well at sea if he isn't worth much upon land.

*   *   *

Irate huntsman (to new groom): 'Look here, confound you! I won't have this! Do you think I'm a fool?'

Sure, sir, I can't say, sir. I only came here yesterday!

Brendan Behan

Brendan Behan used to say that he only took a drink twice a day – when he was thirsty and when he wasn't.

*   *   *

I was born a pet, God love me.

*   *   *

I have never, on my travels, ever met anything worse than myself.

*   *   *

If you don't get up and go down town you'd hear nothing, nor find what they're saying about you. And God send they're saying something. Good or bad, it's better to be criticised than ignored.

*   *   *

The Behans have always had a reputation for the wit. One aunt who lived on the banks of the Canal would invite all and sundry, without even a smile on her lips, to 'drop in anytime you're passin'.

* * *

Brendan was a great man for swimming . . . and he wasn't always worried about the convention of dressing. Once on a crowded beach he ran to the water with not a stitch on, roaring as he went: 'Close your eyes, girls, I'm coming through.'

* * *

When *Borstal Boy* was banned in Ireland he tried to laugh it off and made up his own verse to go to the tune of *Mac-Namara's Band*.

Oh, me name is Brendan Behan, I'm the latest of the banned,
Although we're small in numbers we're the best banned in the land,
We're read at wakes and weddin's and in every parish hall,
And under library counters sure you'll have no trouble at all.

* * *

To go to California and not see Hollywood is like going to Ireland and not seeing the Lakes of Killarney.

*   *   *

When I'm in health I'm not at all religious. But when I'm sick I'm very religious.

*   *   *

There's no bad publicity except an obituary.

*   *   *

John B Keane tells of the time his young son said to Brendan:

Don't drink any more.
Brendan: Whatever you say, Bill, but I'll just have one more to wash the last one down.

*   *   *

If there were only three Irishmen left in the world you'd find two of them in a corner talking about the other. We're a backbiting race.

*   *   *

Brendan was being defended on a charge of entering England illegally. His solicitor apologised for his behaviour and put it down to his being a 'love-child' of the Irish revolution. Said Brendan:

The mother was scandalised, never mind slandered.

* * *

On one occasion Brendan was in on the 'rescue' of an IRA man from Leyhill prison in Surrey. It was Brendan's job after the rescue to guard a Park Ranger near the prison. Said Brendan:

A decent man, A quiet respectable Irishman, who, even though he was employed by the British Imperial Majesty, never spoke a word against us or his parent country. Helpful. Not a bit of trouble. And the only effin thing I did to convince him of our good intentions was to hold a .45 revolver to his head all the time. Cocked.

* * *

Stephen Behan once explained why he did not produce plays like his two sons, Brendan and Dominic:

I've been too busy producing the playwrights.

* * *

'What's the Ascendancy?' someone once asked him, and Brendan replied:

A Protestant on a horse.

Seated one snowy, cold day on the sea wall of the Liffey he saw, passing on the other side of the broad quay, a well-known nature writer whose gentility aroused his vulgarity. He shouted with a roar that almost stopped the traffic:

Hey missus, how's the blue tits?

*   *   *

Wherever Brendan went a large crowd went too and there was always the fellow who 'knew' him. On one occasion a noisy Kerryman shouted: 'We were in the same brigade in the IRA.' Behan sobered up and took a long look at the newcomer.

Go 'long, you bowsie, the only brigade you ever saw was the fire brigade.

* * *

Once in a Dublin pub he was asked for a loan of a fiver by a gentleman with a nose for suckers. But Brendan was having none of it. 'I remember the time, Behan, when you hadn't a light' said the toucher.

That may be, but you don't remember it half as well as I do!

* * *

At the funeral of Lord Longford, Brendan met a friend of other old hard times, Jimmy Hiney. 'I was standing at the gate of the Protestant cemetery wondering whether I should go in or not,' says Jimmy, 'when Brendan came up. Says he:

Jimmy, I think we'll go in and sing a few hymns for the ould * * * *. He has as much a chance of heaven as either of us.'

* * *

For his last quip – looking up at the nun just before he died – he whispered a thank you, and then said:

May you be the mother of a bishop.

John Philpot Curran

John Philpot Curran was an advocate, poet and parliamentarian and also the high priest of Irish repartee. He was born in Newmarket, Cork, on 24th July 1750. After a brilliant career at the Bar he became Master of the Rolls and died in England on 14th October 1817. He was, like most good Corkmen, buried in Glasnevin Cemetery, Dublin.

In a Dublin drawingroom a great number of mediocrities were airing their importance and an intensely national friend informed Curran that there was not a man amongst them who had not had a distinguished ancestor. Curran replied:

Bless my soul, what a crowd of anti-climaxes!

* * *

A blustering Irish barrister once told John Philpot Curran that he would put him in his pocket if he provoked him further:

If you do so, you will have more law in your pocket than you ever had in your head.

*   *   *

A Limerick banker, renowned for his sagacity, had an iron leg. Said Curran:

His leg is the softest thing about him.

*   *   *

Curran, once engaged in legal argument, noticed that behind him stood a barrister, tall and thin, who had originally intended taking Holy Orders. The case was about a question of ecclesiastical law. Curran said to the Judge:

I should refer your Worship to a high authority behind me, who was intended for the church, though in my opinion he was fitter for the steeple.

*   *   *

A wealthy but weak-headed barrister once remarked to Curran that 'No one should be admitted to the Bar who had not an independent landed property.'

May I ask, sir, How many acres make a wiseacre?

* * *

He was one of the few lawyers with a quicker tongue than the 'Hanging Judge' Norbury – and the courage to use it. Norbury was asked at a Bar dinner one day if he would care for some beef.

Norbury: Is it hung?
Curran: Oh, you have only to try it, and it is sure to be hung!

* * *

'If you say another word, I'll commit you,' said an angry judge. To which Curran retorted:

If your lordship shall do so, we shall both of us have the consolation of reflecting that I am not the worst thing that your lordship has committed.

* * *

Judge Fitzgibbon (later Lord Chancellor Clare) in a discussion with Curran in court one day exclaimed rather sharply in reply to some legal point urged by Curran, 'Oh, if that be the law, Mr Curran, I may burn my law books!'

You had better read them, my lord.

On another occasion, the same judge, while Curran was addressing him in a most important case, occupied himself with giving too much attention to a favourite Newfoundland dog seated by him in court. Curran having ceased speaking through indignation, Lord Clare raised his head, and asked: *'Why don't you proceed, Mr Curran?'*

I thought your Lordships were in consultation.

*   *   *

He once said that he could never speak for a quarter of an hour in public without moistening his lips. One of his listeners, Sir Thomas Turton, said: 'I have the advantage on you there, Curran, I spoke the other night for five hours in the House of Commons and never felt in the least thirsty.'

That is very remarkable indeed for everyone agrees that it was the driest speech of the session.

*   *   *

Once told that a slovenly barrister had gone to London with a shirt and a guinea, Curran said:

He'll not change either till he comes back.

*   *   *

A witness, breaking down under the deadly cross-questioning of Curran, complained to the judge that the lawyer confused him. Curran remarked:

Yes, a confusion of the head arising from a corruption of the heart.

*   *   *

He once referred to an individual who took himself too seriously as:

Being afraid to smile lest anyone might suppose that he was too familiar with himself.

*   *   *

'Do you see anything ridiculous in my wig?' asked a vain barrister whose displaced wig had caused some merriment in court.

Nothing, except your head.

*   *   *

A few mornings before Curran's death a doctor observed to him that he coughed very badly.

That's strange, for I've been practising all night.

Dean Jonathan Swift

Ambition often puts men upon doing the meanest offices; so climbing is performed in the same posture with creeping.

* * *

Lady Carteret, wife of the Lord Lieutenant of Ireland, praising Ireland said to Swift: 'Sir, the air of your country is healthy and very excellent.' He replied:

For God's sake, madam, don't say so in England; for if you do they will certainly tax it.

* * *

Observation is an old man's memory.

* * *

When a true Genius appears in the world you may know him by this sign, that the Dunces are all in Confederacy against him.

*　　　*　　　*

'I propose,' said Swift to a group of friends, 'that a tax be levied on female beauty.'
'But, sir,' objected a listener, 'could we ever make women pay enough to make such a tax levy worth while?'
'That would be the least of our difficulties,' laughed Swift. 'Let every woman be permitted to assess her own charms — then she'll be generous enough.'

*　　　*　　　*

He was once accosted by a drunken weaver.

Weaver: I've been spinning it.
Swift: Aye, and reeling it home.

*　　　*　　　*

A lawyer was dining with Swift and, hoping to make a joke with the Dean, asked: 'Suppose, doctor, that the parsons and the devil went to law, which, in your opinion, would win the case?'

The devil would. All the lawyers and attorneys would be on his side.

*　　　*　　　*

Good manners is the art of making those people easy with whom we converse. Whoever makes the fewest people uneasy, is the best bred in the company.

* * *

When I was young I thought all the world, as well as myself, was wholly taken up in discoursing upon the last new play.

* * *

I never knew any man who came to greatness and eminence who lay in bed in the morning.

* * *

Some of Swift's resolutions for when he got old:

Not to marry a young woman.
Not to keep young company, unless they really desire it.
Not to be peevish, or morose, or suspicious.
Not to be fond of children.
Not to boast of my former beauty or favour with ladies.
Not to harken to flatteries, or believe I can be beloved by a young woman – *and finally:*
Not to set up for observing all these rules for fear I should observe none.

* * *

Once presented with beef which was overdone, Swift called the cook and told her to take it downstairs and cook it less. 'I cannot, sir,' replied the bewildered servant.

Why, what sort of creature are you, to commit a fault that cannot be mended?'

* * *

He could not bear lies and when anyone tried to cover up after telling a lie he admonished him:

Come, come, don't attempt to darn your cobwebs.

Wisdom is a fox, who, after long hunting, will at last cost you the pains to dig it out; it is a cheese, which, by how much the richer, has the thicker, the homelier, and the coarser coat, and whereof to a judicious palate the maggots are the best; it is a sack-posset, wherein the deeper you go you will find it the sweeter. Wisdom is a hen, whose cackling we must value and consider, because it is attended with an egg; but then, lastly, it is a nut, which, unless you choose with judgment, may cost you a tooth, and pay you with nothing but a worm.

*　　*　　*

Very few men, properly speaking, live at present, but are providing to live another time.

*　　*　　*

The last thing Swift wrote was an epigram on the building of a magazine for arms and stores. This was pointed out to him as he was taking exercise in the Phoenix Park, during his mental troubles.

> Behold a proof of Irish sense;
> Here Irish wit is seen;
> When nothing's left that's worth defence,
> They build a magazine.

Wilde Words

Oscar Fingall O'Flahertie Wills Wilde (1854–1900).
A man whose words were designed to shock the intellect
rather than the feelings: A hothouse of words.

Missionaries are the divinely provided food for destitute and
underfed cannibals. Whenever they are on the brink of
starvation, Heaven in its infinite mercy sends them a nice
plump missionary.

* * *

I sometimes think that God in creating man somewhat over-
estimated His ability.

* * *

A man can be happy with any woman as long as he does not
love her.

* * *

Wilde loved his food:

To make a good salad, is to be a brilliant diplomatist – the problem is the same in both cases. To know exactly how much oil to put with one's vinegar.

*   *   *

At a party, a chicken was put before him to carve. After several attempts he turned to his wife and said:

Constance, why do you give me these . . . pedestrians . . . to eat?

*   *   *

It is only an auctioneer who can equally and impartially admire all schools of art.

*   *   *

The discovery of America was the beginning of the death of art.

*   *   *

Perhaps after all America has never been discovered. I myself would merely say that it has been detected.

*   *   *

A bad man is the sort of man who admires innocence and a bad woman is the sort of woman a man never gets tired of.

*   *   *

Someone asked Wilde: 'Do you know George Moore?'

Do I know him, is it? Yes I know him so well I have not spoken to him for ten years. . . .

*   *   *

George Moore said of him:

Wilde paraphrased and inverted the witticisms and epigrams of others. His method of literary piracy was on the lines of the robber Cacus, who dragged stolen cows backwards by the tails into his cavern so that their hoofprints might not lead to detection.

*   *   *

Always forgive your enemies; nothing annoys them so much.

*   *   *

Oh, he (my brother) often takes an alcoholiday.

*   *   *

Wilde said when he went to America he had two secretaries – one for autographs, the other for locks of hair. Within six months the one had died of writer's cramp, the other was completely bald.

* * *

He met a woman in Paris who took a pride in her ugliness. 'Don't you think,' she asked him, 'that I am the ugliest woman in Paris?'

No – in all the world.

* * *

Wilde had two views about high society – early on he loved it, later he despised it. Commenting on it he said:

To get into the best society nowadays one has either to feed people, amuse people, or shock people – that is all.

* * *

The one charm of marriage is that it makes life a deception absolutely necessary for both parties.

When a woman marries again it is because she detested her first husband. When a man marries again it is because he adored his first wife.

It is a curious thing about the game of marriage – the wives hold all the honours and invariably lose the odd trick.

Married life is merely a habit.

In married households the champagne is rarely of a first rate brand.

Men marry because they are tired; women because they are curious; both are disappointed.

*   *   *

Crying is the refuge of plain women but the ruin of pretty ones.

Women treat us just as humanity treats its gods. They worship us and are always bothering us to do something for them.

Talk to every woman as if you loved her, and to every man as if he bored you.

Women's styles may change but their designs remain the same.

*   *   *

The young are always ready to give those who are older than themselves the full benefit of their inexperience.

*   *   *

In America life is one long expectoration.

*   *   *

Teach the English how to talk and the Irish how to listen; then society will be quite civilised.

*   *   *

The English think that a cheque can solve every problem in life.

*   *   *

It is better to take pleasure in a rose than to put its root under a microscope.

*   *   *

Speaking of a man Wilde said:

He hasn't a single redeeming vice.

*   *   *

Work is the curse of the drinking classes.

*   *   *

Experience is the name which everyone gives to his mistakes.

*   *   *

The English have a miraculous power of turning wine into water.

* * *

He was seldom rude to anyone but on one occasion a certain nobleman clapped him exuberantly on the back as he was speaking: 'Why Oscar, you are getting fatter and fatter.' Wilde replied:

And you are getting ruder and ruder.

* * *

Once, going through Trinity College, Wilde met an undergraduate and asked him to accompany him home:

I want to introduce you to my mother. We have founded a society for the suppression of virtue.

* * *

Wilde prophesied:

I'll be a poet, a writer, a dramatist. Somehow or other I'll be famous, and if not famous, notorious.

* * *

André Gide once criticised Wilde's plays. Wilde listened intently and then said:

I put all my genius into my life; I only put my talent into my works.

*   *   *

Before he died, Wilde said that he was dying as he had lived – beyond his means.

Dying . . . and Beyond

An Irishman was opposed to building a new wall around a grave-yard because:

Those outside don't want to get in and those inside can't get out.

* * *

When Lord Palmerston was told he was dying he looked at the doctor and said:

Why, dying is the last thing I shall do.

* * *

An undertaker found a donkey lying dead in front of his premises, and went to inform the police. He asked the officer in charge:

What'll I do with it?
Do with it? Bury it, of course. You're an undertaker, aren't you?

Certainly I am, but I thought I should come round and inform the relatives first.

*   *   *

Johnny Patterson, the famous Irish clown, lay critically ill. The doctor, having done all he could, closed his medicine case and prepared to leave: 'I'll see you in the morning, Johnny,' he said cheerfully. Instinctively, the dying clown smirked, gave his eye a professional roll that had helped launch many a quip, and murmured:

Sure, doc, but will I see you?

*   *   *

'*If the devil was to come here now,*' asked the Englishman, '*which of us do you think he'd take?*'

Galwayman: He'd take me.
Why do you think so?
Because he'd be sure of yourself anytime.

*   *   *

After an oration at the graveside of a famous writer an old woman was heard to say:

Wasn't it worth his while to die to have the like o'that said about him!

*   *   *

Belfast playwright Joe Tomelty said:

If there's music in hell it'll be the bagpipes.

*   *   *

The Ulsterman had just been told by a clergyman of the death of an inveterate enemy. 'Well,' he said, 'it's a comfort to know that the devil's got that fellow at last.' The clergyman protested against this uncharitable view, to which the Ulsterman replied:

Well, if the devil hasn't got that fellow, all I can say is that I don't see much use in us keeping a devil at all.

*　　*　　*

A letter writer to the 'Irish Times':
As I was passing a ninety-five per cent female Bingo queue in the city recently, an evening funeral procession approached. I stood in unconcerned respect and as I did so, a middle-aged lady detached herself from the queue. She knelt down upon one knee, and striking her pendulous Dublin bosom three times, murmured 'Mercy, mercy, mercy!' Having rejoined the waiting line her neighbour asked, 'Why did you kneel?' To which she replied:

Why wouldn't I? – wasn't he a good husband to me?

*　　*　　*

An Irishman writing a letter of condolence to the widow of a late colleague said:

I cannot tell you how sorry I was to hear that your husband has gone to heaven. We were great friends and it is sad to think that we will never meet again.

*　　*　　*

The Belfast doctor's waiting-room was very full. Every chair was taken and some patients were standing. There was desultory conversation, but after a while a silence fell and the patients sat waiting. Finally, an old man stood up wearily and remarked:

Ach, I think I'll go home and die a natural death.

* * *

The farmer looking at the loitering labourer:

You'd be a good messenger to send for death.

* * *

Guide, to visitors, after showing them around the graveyard:

If God spares me, I shall be here myself some day.

Words of Wisdom

A politician's view:

The great difference between England and Ireland is that in England you can say what you like as long as you do the right thing; in Ireland you can do what you like as long as you say the right thing.

* * *

Lord Brabazon of Tara:

Always behave like a duck – keep calm and unruffled on the surface, but paddle like the devil underneath.

* * *

A skinny and pensive James Joyce was sitting on the wall of a swimming bath during a gala. 'Who are you representing?' asked an official. With mock sorrow Joyce replied:

Hunger.

* * *

Judge Eugene Sheehy recorded that James Joyce's father was at breakfast one morning and read an obituary notice of a dear friend, Mrs Cassidy. Mrs Joyce was shocked and cried out:

Oh! Don't tell me that Mrs Cassidy is dead!
Well I don't quite know about that, but someone has taken
    the liberty of burying her.

*　　*　　*

Sean O'Casey:

Life: A lament in one ear and a song in the other.

*　　*　　*

Patrick Kavanagh:

One of the reasons why I consider Mahomet a poor prophet – meaning poor poet – was his deciding to go to the mountain when it refused to come to him. If he had been a good poet he would have walked the other way and the mountain would keep following him for ever.

*　　*　　*

Robert Lynd:

To see a policeman running is, I think, next to hearing a declaration of war, the most exciting experience of which a human being is capable.

*　　*　　*

Oliver Goldsmith:

The wise are polite all the world over – but fools are polite only at home.

*   *   *

The famous entertainer, Val Vousden, once asked a circus master, who was playing the same town, to give their historical drama 'Robert Emmet' a boost. The ringmaster was delighted to help and announced during the evening:

If you want to see how Ireland has suffered and is suffering still, go and see Val Vousden play Robert Emmet!

*   *   *

Tom Kettle, Redmondite MP, Professor of Economics, was a wit as well as a philosopher:

Life is a cheap *table d'hôte* in a rather dirty restaurant, with time changing the plates before you have had enough of anything.

It is with ideas, as with umbrellas; if left lying about they are peculiarly liable to a change of ownership.

At a public dinner it is not so much the menu that matters as the man you sit next to.

Philosophy is a blanket which men have woven to protect themselves from life.

Tyranny is worse than a crime – it is an extravagance.

*　　*　　*

Richard Brinsley Sheridan:

I must – I will – I can – I ought – I do.

*　　*　　*

Sheridan, who was always in money troubles, was asked by a creditor to pay at least the interest on the money he owed. He replied:

My dear fellow, it is not in my interest to pay the principle or in my principle to pay the interest.

*　　*　　*

Sir Samuel Ferguson, the Belfast-born poet and antiquarian, visited Rath Cruaghan in Roscommon. He discussed the cromlech builders with the father of the famous entertainer, Percy French. Old Mr French remarked:

How a monolith, weighing one hundred tons, could be placed on pillars twelve feet high without the aid of machinery, I can't conceive.

Sir Samuel: An inclined plane, one thousand men all pulling the same way would do it.

Old Mr French: Granted, but where in Ireland would you find one thousand men all pulling the same way?

* * *

During an argument with a colleague on corporal punishment in schools, Professor J P Mahaffy was declaiming against the practice on the grounds that, when once inflicted, the damage could not be remedied. 'The only time I ever was swished,' said the Professor, 'was for telling the truth.'

Well, Mahaffy, it was effective in your case, for it certainly cured you.

Mahaffy had his own brand of wit:

In Ireland the inevitable never happens, but the unexpected often occurs.

An Irish atheist is one who wishes to God he could believe in God.

Asked the difference between a man and a woman, his instant reply was:

I cannot conceive.

* * *

William Butler Yeats:

My father used to say, that the great difference between England and Ireland is that every Englishman has rich relations and every Irishman poor ones.

Nobody running at full speed has either a head or a heart.

They [the English] insist in presenting us with all the good qualities they do not want for themselves.

*   *   *

George Moore:

My one claim to originality among Irishmen is that I have never made a speech.

A wonderful race is the race of women; they're misunderstood by men, for they understand only lovers, children and flowers.

All reformers are bachelors.

*   *   *

Lynn Doyle:

If you want to reach the age of eighty-five, get a stomach ulcer when you're twenty-five, and you'll take such good care of yourself, for fear of upsetting the ulcer, that you'll outlast all around you.

Life would be a nobler thing if we avoided petty tittle-tattle about our neighbours but the evenings would be terribly long.

* * *

Patrick Campbell writing in My Life and Easy Times *says:*

I place great faith in my own anonymity. It's only if you go to the office so that they can see what they've hired, that you're likely to get the sack.

* * *

Sean Dunne, TD:

The Cabinet is said to be the youngest in Europe, but I sometimes detect signs of premature senility.

* * *

A well-known politician:

The ways of Providence are indeed unscrupulous.

*　　*　　*

Candidate at election meeting, 'Now friends what do we need to carry this constituency to the biggest majority in the history of Fianna Fail?

Another candidate!

*　　*　　*

An Irish TD:

This country would die if it didn't have a grievance.

*　　*　　*

A Derryman:

There's two classes of boys that need to have good memories – liars and politicians.

*　　*　　*

Professor Robert Yelverton Tyrrell always raged when he saw a sign saying 'Temperance Hotel'. He would tell the proprietor:

There is no such thing, you might as well talk of a celibate brothel.

*   *   *

Bernard Shaw once made a personal appearance at the end of one of his plays. When the general applause had subsided, one man began to hiss. Shaw immediately pointed his finger at the man:

I quite agree with you, my friend, it is a rotten play. But what are we among so many?

Bernard Shaw's flowing beard was long a topic of conversation. One day, at an interview, a reporter asked him: 'What made you grow a beard?' 'Vanity,' confessed Shaw, 'but common sense made me retain it.'

Reporter: How is that?
Well, in all these years, I've probably written several plays in the time I would have spent shaving.

*   *   *

In the foyer of the Cork House after the première of one of his plays, a lady with an umbrella stopped J B Keane and berated him publicly. 'Stand there', she shouted, prodding him with the umbrella, 'till I give you a piece of my mind.'

My dear woman your mind is so small that if you give me a bit of it you wouldn't have any left for yourself.

* * *

The tourist had seen the Devil's Gap, the Devil's Glen, the Devil's Pot and remarked to the man in charge of the tour: 'The devil owns a lot of land in Ireland; he must be an important man.'

You're right, but like all the landlords his home is in England.

* * *

An Irishman was explaining to some friends that he thought he saw a ghost one night and took up his gun and shot it. When he got up in the morning he found it was only his shirt. 'What did you do then?' asked his friend.

I knelt down and thanked God I was not in it.

* * *

The foreman was annoyed when he saw that a new wall had been laid crooked. He criticised his bricklayer and pointed out the spot where it twisted. The bricklayer replied:

It's right, you are, bad luck to the fella Lynch, he never sold a straight piece of string in his life.

*   *   *

A man had undergone a rather serious operation in a Dublin nursing home. When he 'came out' of the anaesthetic he found that although it was broad daylight the blind of his window was fully drawn. He accosted the surgeon who was standing at his bedside. 'Why on earth is the blind drawn?'

Well, it so happens that the house across the road is on fire; and I was afraid that if you saw it when you woke up you might conclude that the operation had not been a success.

*   *   *

A famous landlord was renowned for late rising, usually taking his breakfast when the rest of the family were having lunch. Asked one day to account for his habit he replied:

The fact is I sleep very slowly.

*   *   *

A Dublin firm sent the following letter to customers whose accounts were overdue:

Man is dust. Dust settles. Be a man.

I hand my pay packet to the wife every week, but I think she'd rather have the money.' THE BAMBA REVIEW, AUGUST, 1967

A Meath farmer's wife collected five thousand pounds insurance on her husband's death. When she was being presented with the cheque she sighed:

Oh, dear, I'd give a thousand pounds to have my poor, dear husband back.

*   *   *

A man had been trying for a job but was continually being turned down at the local factory. One day in exasperation he said:

When you have plenty of work you give it to others; when you have none you give it to me.

* * *

Note from a girl at boarding-school for the first time:

This is really a lovely school. All our teachers are certified.

* * *

A Frenchman claiming for his country the invention of all the elegances, named among other things the ruffee, the Irishman answered:

We went one better – we put the shirt on it.

* * *

Someone threw a head of cabbage at an Irish politician while he was making a speech. He paused a second, and said:

Gentlemen, I only ask for your ears, I don't care for your heads!

* * *

An Irishman gave two reasons for talking to himself:

First he always liked to talk to a sensible man; secondly he always liked to hear a sensible man talk.

*   *   *

The Dublin man was coming back from a trip to Belfast and was stopped at a border post. 'Have you any pornographic literature with you?' asked the Customs man.

Sure what in hell would I be doing with that; sure I haven't even a pornagraph to play it on.

Definitions and Proverbs

Alcohol: A liquid for preserving almost everything but secrets. (*The Pioneer*)

*   *   *

Drunk: When a man feels sophisticated but can't pronounce it. (*The Pioneer*)

*   *   *

The perfect age for children: Too old to cry at night and too young to borrow the car. (*Tatler* in the *Irish Independent*)

*   *   *

An Irish beggar's coat: A bundle of holes sewn together.

*   *   *

Success: The only infallible criterion of wisdom to vulgar judgment.   (*Edmund Burke*)

*　　*　　*

Bachelor: A man who shirkes responsibility and duties.
                                        (*George Bernard Shaw*)

*　　*　　*

Failure: The path of least resistance.

*　　*　　*

Hobby: Hard work that you would be ashamed to do for a living.

*　　*　　*

Tolerance: The suspicion that the other fellow might be right.

*　　*　　*

Horse-power: Something that was much safer when only horses had it.

*　　*　　*

Memory: Something a man forgets with when he owes you money.

*　　*　　*

Antique: Something no one would be seen with if there were more of them, but which everyone wants when no one has any.

*　　*　　*

Soil: That from which farmers and laundries make a living.

(*Farmers' Journal*)

*　　*　　*

Laughter: The chorus of conversation.

*　　*　　*

Average Woman: One who is always a wish ahead of her budget.　　　　　　　　　　　　　　　　　(*Irish Echo*)

*　　*　　*

Ocean: Huge body of water surrounded entirely by rumours of everlasting peace.

*　　*　　*

The horse: A friend of man so long as man doesn't bet on him.   (*Dublin Opinion*)

* * *

The Impossible: Building a barrel round a bung hole.

* * *

Nonsense: Bolting a door with a boiled carrot.

* * *

Marriage: A pair of shears that cannot be separated, often moving in opposite directions, yet always punishing whatever comes between them.

* * *

A pessimist: A woman driver who's afraid she won't be able to squeeze her car into a very small parking space. An optimist is a man who believes she won't try.

* * *

An Irishman's description of an American:

He'd kiss a queen till he'd raise a blister,
With his arms round her neck, and his old felt hat on;
Address a king by the title of Mister,
And ask him the price of the throne he sat on.

* * *

Friends: Thermometers by which we may judge the temperature of our fortune.   (*Countess of Blessington*)

*   *   *

A super salesman: A man who sells something he hasn't got to people who don't want it.

*   *   *

It's a lonely washing that hasn't a man's shirt in it.

*   *   *

You've got to do your own growing no matter how tall your grandfather was.

*   *   *

Never put your hand out further than you can draw it back again.

*   *   *

In wealth, many friends. In poverty not even relatives.

*   *   *

Keep your eyes wide open before marriage and half shut afterwards.

*   *   *

He is a wise man who has his afterthoughts first.

*   *   *

Give a boy and a pig everything they want. You'll get a good pig and a bad boy.

*   *   *

Far off cows have long horns.

*'Well, I'll go, oul son, I won't
take up any more of your time!'*

He breaks his wife's head and then buys a plaster for it.

*   *   *

A shoemaker's wife and a smith's mare are always badly shod.

*   *   *

A watched pot never boils.

*   *   *

He improves – like bad fish in July.

*   *   *

The man that was born to be hanged need never fear water.

*   *   *

He'd skin a flea for its hide and tallow.

*   *   *

If you have a cow you can always find someone to milk her.

*   *   *

Never take for a wife a woman who has no faults.

*   *   *

One who lies down with dogs will get up with fleas.

*   *   *

A good word never broke a tooth.

*   *   *

Do not tell your troubles to one who has no pity.

*   *   *

Three things a man can never fathom:

A woman's mind.
The work of the bees.
The ebb and flow of the tides.

*   *   *

Acknowledgements

Acknowledgements for material used in a collection of this kind have to be extensive and I trust that all those who loaned me their words will accept my gratitude. In most cases, I have been able to give credit with the witticism in the relevant chapter, but many other people gave me a great deal of help. Particularly I would like to thank the Chief Librarian of Dublin, Miss Mairin O'Byrne and her assistants, Miss Dowd and Miss Burke; and the Chief Librarian of Dun Laoghaire, Mr Casey, and his assistants, Miss Doyle and Miss O'Connor. Many editors and writers gave me access to their own personal collections, while Mr Charles Kelly, editor of *Dublin Opinion*, put his complete files at my disposal. All these I add to my list of credits. Any omissions will, I trust, be forgiven.

SMcC